There Shall Be No Needy

Teacher's Guide

Pursuing Social Justice

through

Jewish Law & Tradition

RABBI JILL JACOBS

The complete teacher's guide to
*There Shall Be No Needy: Pursuing Social Justice
through Jewish Law & Tradition* by Rabbi Jill Jacobs

Other Social Justice Resources from Jewish Lights

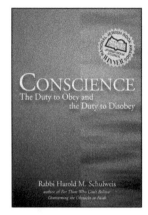

Conscience
The Duty to Obey and the Duty to Disobey
By Rabbi Harold M. Schulweis

Provocative. Examines the idea of conscience and the role it plays in our relationships to law, ethics, religion, human nature and God—and to each other. Winner of the National Jewish Book Award.

6 x 9, 160 pp, Quality PB, 978-1-58023-419-1
Hardcover, 978-1-58023-375-0

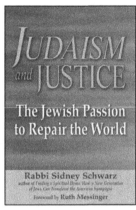

Judaism and Justice
The Jewish Passion to Repair the World
By Rabbi Sidney Schwarz
Foreword by Ruth W. Messinger

Explores Judaism, social justice and the Jewish identity of American Jews.

6 x 9, 352 pp, Quality PB, 978-1-58023-353-8
Hardcover, 978-1-58023-312-5

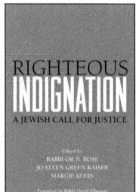

Righteous Indignation
A Jewish Call for Justice
Edited by Rabbi Or N. Rose, Jo Ellen Green Kaiser and Margie Klein
Foreword by Rabbi David Ellenson, PhD

Leading progressive Jewish activists explore meaningful intellectual and spiritual foundations upon which to base social justice work.

6 x 9, 384 pp, Quality PB, 978-1-58023-414-6
Hardcover, 978-1-58023-336-1

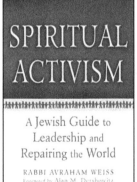

Spiritual Activism
A Jewish Guide to Leadership and Repairing the World
By Rabbi Avraham Weiss
Foreword by Alan M. Dershowitz

This provocative and challenging guidebook will show you how to be proactive in repairing our broken world—and so much more.

6 x 9, 224 pp, Quality PB, 978-1-58023-418-4
Hardcover, 978-1-58023-355-2

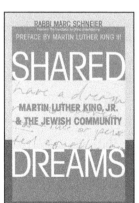

Shared Dreams
Martin Luther King, Jr. & the Jewish Community
By Rabbi Marc Schneier
Preface by Martin Luther King III

Brings to life the impressive, surprising and long-neglected history of Martin Luther King, Jr.'s efforts in support of the Jewish community.

6 x 9, 240 pp, Quality PB, 978-1-58023-273-9

There Shall Be No Needy

Teacher's Guide

Pursuing Social Justice
through
Jewish Law & Tradition

RABBI JILL JACOBS

JEWISH LIGHTS Publishing

ISBN-13: 978-1-58023-429-0 (pbk.)
ISBN-13: 978-1-68336-460-3 (hardcover)

Published by Jewish Lights Publishing
www.jewishlights.com

CONTENTS

HOW TO USE THIS TEACHER'S GUIDE

I wrote *There Shall Be No Needy: Pursuing Social Justice through Jewish Law and Tradition* with the goal of transforming the Jewish discourse around social justice. I intended for this book to be a guide to creating a three-way conversation among Jewish text, real-life social and economic concerns, and contemporary public policy thinking, as well as an inspiration to act on pressing issues. In the months since publication, I have been thrilled to hear from rabbis, educators, and activists who are using the book to spark conversation within Jewish communities about policy issues, to add a Jewish dimension to ongoing social justice work, and to educate themselves and others about the ways that Jewish text and tradition might inform our engagement with the world.

I have also received many requests for a teacher's guide to assist rabbis, professors, and other educators in using *There Shall Be No Needy: Pursuing Social Justice through Jewish Law and Tradition* in adult education, university, and advanced high school classes. I hope that this guide will prove useful in this regard.

This guide is organized sequentially according to the chapters of *There Shall Be No Needy: Pursuing Social Justice through Jewish Law and Tradition*. For each chapter, I offer one trigger exercise aimed at drawing out the participant's own experience with and thinking about the subject at hand. Following the trigger exercise are a number of key texts from the relevant chapter, along with suggested discussion questions about these texts. I then offer some general discussion questions about the chapter as a whole. In the context of a course, you might choose either to first assign the relevant book chapter, and then use the texts to spark more in-depth discussion, or to first study the texts, and then read the book chapter for insight on applying these texts to contemporary situations.

All Bible translations are taken from the Jewish Publication Society's *Tanakh* (Philadelphia: Jewish Publication Society, 1985), though some have been modified for gender neutrality. Unless otherwise indicated, all other translations are my own.

The biblical Hebrew text includes vowels, for ease of reading. Rabbinic, medieval, and modern Hebrew texts are generally not printed with vowels, so I have followed this convention in this teacher's guide.

I hope that this guide sparks interesting conversations in your classrooms and communities, and that these conversations, in turn, inspire your communities to action. I look forward to hearing about the results.

INTRODUCTION

The Search for an Integrated Judaism

Goals

- Participants will be able to identify the source(s) of their own connections to social justice work.
- Participants will understand some of the different reasons that Jews give for their own social justice work.

Trigger Exercise

1. Below, you will find ten statements that describe why some Jews feel compelled to do social justice work. Photocopy each statement on a separate piece of paper, enlarging each as much as possible. Alternatively, you may write each statement on a poster board or other large piece of paper. Hang these pieces of paper around the room.
2. Ask participants to walk around the room, read each statement, and then stand next to the statement that they find most compelling. You should acknowledge that it will be difficult to choose only one statement, but that for the sake of the conversation, participants should commit to only one.
3. Give participants a few minutes to walk around and choose their statement. When everyone has chosen a statement, go around the room and ask one volunteer from each statement group to read the first line of their selected statement, and then to explain why he or she finds this statement compelling.
4. Ask participants to find a partner who chose a different statement. Once every participant has found a partner, ask the pairs to talk about the following questions:
   a. Why did you find this statement compelling? Does this statement reflect your own approach to social justice work? How or how not?
   b. Were there other statements to which you also felt drawn? Why?
   c. Were there other statements that you found entirely uncompelling or even offensive? Why?
5. Bring the group back together and ask a few volunteers to share any insights or questions that emerged from their conversations. Did they learn anything from their part-

ners? Did anything in the conversation surprise them? Do they have additional questions about why Jews might choose to do social justice work?

Statements

1. The Jewish people have suffered injustice. In our lifetimes and those of our parents and grandparents, we have been the victims of individual and institutional anti-Semitism. We have forgotten neither the atrocities of the Holocaust nor the exclusionary policies of the early twentieth century nor the individual acts of anti-Semitism that continue today. We know that discrimination against any minority threatens all minorities.

2. We share a communal narrative that reminds us of our enslavement to Pharaoh, and of our liberation from Egypt. Rather than use this memory as an excuse to oppress others, we have learned from the experience of oppression an obligation to protect the most vulnerable. Time and again, the Torah reminds us that our personal experience of being strangers instills in us a responsibility toward those in our own society who are at risk for discrimination and oppression.

3. We have been leaders in the major justice battles of the last century. We were among the leaders of the American labor movement, the civil rights movement, and the feminist movement, and we were disproportionately represented among the leaders of the Russian revolution and the early communist and socialist movements. Our revolutionary history has taught us to aspire to be leaders in creating long-term change.

4. We have long been the go-betweens, and have experienced both the benefits and the risks of this position. As merchants, we moved between different places and cultures, learning new perspectives on the world, and accustoming ourselves to getting along with many types of people. In the role of the court Jew, we enjoyed access to power, but also suffered when this position made us the targets of hatred.

5. We view *tzedakah* as a matter of justice. We consider ourselves not to be owners of the land, but rather stewards of the world's resources. In that regard, we are committed to ensuring the well-being of those in need, and to redistributing the money and resources entrusted to us in a more equitable way.

6. We believe that all human beings are equal, unique, and infinitely valuable creations in the divine image. The Talmud teaches that God created all of humanity from a single person "so that no one can say to another 'my father was greater than yours'... if a person makes many coins from one mold, they all look alike, but God fashioned every person in the stamp of the first, and yet not one of them resembles another; therefore every single person is obliged to say, 'the world was created for my sake'" (Mishnah, *Sanhedrin* 4:5).

7. We are the inheritors of a legal system that teaches us ethical interpersonal practices, not only ritual practices. From our tradition, we learn how to create equitable and mutually responsible relationships between workers and employers, landlords and tenants, buyers and sellers, and others between whom there is often an unequal distribution of power.

8. We have heard from the biblical prophets a direct call to be agents of justice. In the Haftarah read each year on Yom Kippur, Isaiah admonishes the people for pursuing business dealings while feigning piety by fasting. Instead, Isaiah says, fasting should provoke empathy with those who are suffering, and should lead to "let[ting] the oppressed go free … deal[ing] your bread to the hungry, and bring[ing] the homeless poor into your house" (Isaiah 58:6–7).

9. We believe in and work toward a perfected world. From our mystical tradition, we have learned that human beings have the power to return the world to its original perfection. Even in the darkest of days, we maintain faith in our own ability to contribute to the ultimate redemption of the world.

10. We recognize that our own fate is bound up in the fate of others. During the 1960s, we joined the civil rights movement in part because we stood to gain from the dismantling of restrictive covenants and quotas. We continue to work on issues such as health care, education, and the environment that have a direct impact on our lives and on the lives of our children, and recognize that we will be most effective when we partner with other communities that share our own economic and social interests.

Statements written by Rabbi Jill Jacobs and Simon Greer for Jewish Funds for Justice.

Discussion Questions for Introduction: The Search for an Integrated Judaism

1. Rabbi Jill Jacobs speaks about the disconnect she once experienced between her Jewish life and her social justice commitments. Have you ever experienced this kind of disconnect? In what context? How can/did you reconcile these two parts of your life?

2. Rabbi Jacobs draws a contrast between the closed space of her rabbinical school and the wider community outside of the building. Why do you think she puts so much emphasis on these spatial constructions? How might your own geographical placement affect your relationships with the world?

3. The Jewish community has a long history of involvement in social justice work, and most synagogues are active in local volunteer projects or—in some cases—advocacy. There are also an increasing number of local and national organizations that involve Jews in social justice work.

4. In what Jewish communal social justice activities have you participated in? How did it feel to do this work as part of a Jewish community, as opposed to as part of a secular organization?

1

A Vision of Economic Justice

Goal

- Participants will understand a Jewish approach to the relationship between the poor and the wealthy.

Trigger Exercise

1. Divide participants into groups of three to five.
2. Give each group five minutes to prepare a human sculpture that, to them, represents the experience of poverty in America. Participants should decide together what image they wish to convey, and should prepare a group pose that will represent this image.
3. Bring the participants back together. Ask each small group, in turn, to present its sculpture, while the rest of the participants look on.
4. Ask participants to reflect on the sculptures they have seen. What feelings did these sculptures provoke? What did the sculptures have in common? What were the differences? What images surprised them?

Text Study

1. Deuteronomy 15:1–11

אמִקֵּץ שֶׁבַע-שָׁנִים, תַּעֲשֶׂה שְׁמִטָּה. בוְזֶה, דְּבַר הַשְּׁמִטָּה—שָׁמוֹט כָּל-בַּעַל מַשֵּׁה
יָדוֹ, אֲשֶׁר יַשֶּׁה בְּרֵעֵהוּ: לֹא-יִגֹּשׂ אֶת-רֵעֵהוּ וְאֶת-אָחִיו, כִּי-קָרָא שְׁמִטָּה לַיהוָה. ג
אֶת-הַנָּכְרִי, תִּגֹּשׂ; וַאֲשֶׁר יִהְיֶה לְךָ אֶת-אָחִיךָ, תַּשְׁמֵט יָדֶךָ. דאֶפֶס, כִּי לֹא יִהְיֶה-
בְּךָ אֶבְיוֹן: כִּי-בָרֵךְ יְבָרֶכְךָ, יְהוָה, בָּאָרֶץ, אֲשֶׁר יְהוָה אֱלֹהֶיךָ נֹתֵן-לְךָ נַחֲלָה
לְרִשְׁתָּהּ. הרַק אִם-שָׁמוֹעַ תִּשְׁמַע, בְּקוֹל יְהוָה אֱלֹהֶיךָ, לִשְׁמֹר לַעֲשׂוֹת אֶת-כָּל-
הַמִּצְוָה הַזֹּאת, אֲשֶׁר אָנֹכִי מְצַוְּךָ הַיּוֹם. וכִּי-יְהוָה אֱלֹהֶיךָ בֵּרַכְךָ, כַּאֲשֶׁר דִּבֶּר-לָךְ;
וְהַעֲבַטְתָּ גּוֹיִם רַבִּים, וְאַתָּה לֹא תַעֲבֹט, וּמָשַׁלְתָּ בְּגוֹיִם רַבִּים, וּבְךָ לֹא יִמְשֹׁלוּ.

זכִּי-יִהְיֶה בְךָ אֶבְיוֹן מֵאַחַד אַחֶיךָ, בְּאַחַד שְׁעָרֶיךָ, בְּאַרְצְךָ, אֲשֶׁר-יְהוָה אֱלֹהֶיךָ נֹתֵן
לָךְ—לֹא תְאַמֵּץ אֶת-לְבָבְךָ, וְלֹא תִקְפֹּץ אֶת-יָדְךָ, מֵאָחִיךָ, הָאֶבְיוֹן. חכִּי-פָתֹחַ
תִּפְתַּח אֶת-יָדְךָ, לוֹ; וְהַעֲבֵט, תַּעֲבִיטֶנּוּ, דֵּי מַחְסֹרוֹ, אֲשֶׁר יֶחְסַר לוֹ. טהִשָּׁמֶר לְךָ
פֶּן-יִהְיֶה דָבָר עִם-לְבָבְךָ בְלִיַּעַל לֵאמֹר, קָרְבָה שְׁנַת-הַשֶּׁבַע שְׁנַת הַשְּׁמִטָּה, וְרָעָה
עֵינְךָ בְּאָחִיךָ הָאֶבְיוֹן, וְלֹא תִתֵּן לוֹ; וְקָרָא עָלֶיךָ אֶל-יְהוָה, וְהָיָה בְךָ חֵטְא. ינָתוֹן
תִּתֵּן לוֹ, וְלֹא-יֵרַע לְבָבְךָ בְּתִתְּךָ לוֹ: כִּי בִּגְלַל הַדָּבָר הַזֶּה, יְבָרֶכְךָ יְהוָה אֱלֹהֶיךָ,
בְּכָל-מַעֲשֶׂךָ, וּבְכֹל מִשְׁלַח יָדֶךָ. יאכִּי לֹא-יֶחְדַּל אֶבְיוֹן, מִקֶּרֶב הָאָרֶץ; עַל-כֵּן
אָנֹכִי מְצַוְּךָ, לֵאמֹר, פָּתֹחַ תִּפְתַּח אֶת-יָדְךָ לְאָחִיךָ לַעֲנִיֶּךָ וּלְאֶבְיֹנְךָ, בְּאַרְצֶךָ.

Every seventh year you shall practice remission of debts. This shall be the nature of the remission: every creditor shall forgive the debt that his fellow owes him; he shall not dun his fellow or kinsman, for the remission proclaimed is of Adonai. You may dun the foreigner; but you must remit whatever is due you from your kinspeople.

There shall be no poor among you—since Adonai your God will bless you in the land that Adonai your God is giving you as a hereditary portion—if only you heed Adonai your God and take care to keep all this Instruction that I enjoin upon you this day. For Adonai your God will bless you as God has promised you....

If, however, there is a needy person among you, one of your kinspeople in any of your settlements in the land that Adonai your God is giving you, do not harden your heart and shut your hand against your needy kinsperson. Rather, you must open your hand and lend him sufficient for whatever he needs. Beware lest you harbor the base thought, "The seventh year, the year of remission, is approaching," so that you are mean to your needy kinsman and give him nothing. This person will cry out to Adonai against you, and you will incur guilt. Give to him readily and have no regrets when you do so, for in return Adonai your God will bless you in all your efforts and in all your undertakings. For the poor will never cease from your land, which is why I command you: open your hand to the poor and needy kinsman in your land.

2. Don Isaac Abravanel on Deuteronomy 15

רוצה לומר שיעיין האדם למי יתן כי לא יהיה ענין הצדקה לתת מתנות לעשירים
וכמאמר שלמה עושק דל להרבות לו נותן לעשיר אך למחסור. ועל זה אמר כי
יהיה בך אביון מאחד אחיך באחד שעריך כי הוא לעניותו וחסרונו ראוי לחמול
עליו ויעביטוהו די מחסורו. וכלל בזה שלושה בחינות. האחד מפני חסרונו
שראוי שהאדם אשר נתן לו השם יתברך מטובו יחמול על הצריך אליו. וכמו
שאמרו רבותינו ז"ל בפרק קמא דבבא בתרא (דף ט) האומר פרנסוני שומעים
לו. וזהו אמרם אפס כי לא יהיה בך אביון. והשני מפאת הקורבה אשר לו עמך.
כי הוא זרע אברהם ברוך ולכן ראוי הוא שתסייעהו בעת צרתו. ועל זה אמר
מאחד אחיך. והשלשה מצד השכנות ואהבה.

This means that a person should look into to whom one gives *tzedakah*, for the point of *tzedakah* is not to give gifts to the wealthy, as it says, "The one who oppresses the poor to increase one's own riches, and the one who gives to the poor shall come to want" (Proverbs 22:16). About this, the text says, "If, however, there is a needy person among you, one of your kinsmen in any of your settlements." For, because of this person's poverty and need, it is appropriate to have compassion on him/her and to provide sufficient for this person's need. There are three aspects [to this giving]: First, because of this person's need, it is appropriate for the person to whom the blessed God has given from God's goodness to have compassion on the one who is in need of him/her. As the Rabbis said, "If a person says, 'sustain me,' listen to this person" (Babylonian Talmud, *Bava Batra* 9a). This is what is meant by "There will be no needy among you." Second—because of the closeness which this person has to you. For this person is from the seed of the blessed Abraham, and therefore it is appropriate that you should help this person in the time of his/her need. About this, it says, "One of your kinsmen." And the third reason is because of neighborliness and love.

3. Moshe Alshich on Deuteronomy 15

כי יהיה בך אביון כי בך בשבילך הוא מה שיש אביון למען זכותך בהתפרנס על
ידך.

If there is among you (*b'kha*) a poor person. [This means] "Because of you" (*bishvilkha*). There are poor in order that you should receive merit by supporting them.

4. Isaac Caro, *Tol'dot Yitzchak* on Deuteronomy 15

הסיבה שהעני הוא העשיר, שלפי שכוכב שלך ברום הגלגל כוכב שלו למטה,
ולזה אמר את העני עמך מה צורך לומר עמך אלא לומר הסיבה שהוא עני, ואם
לא תתן לו מה יעשה הקב״ה יתן סביב לגלגל באופן שהכוכב שהוא למעלה
יהיה למטה, ולזה אמר בגלל הדבר הזה.

The reason that the poor person is poor is because the rich person is rich; when your star ascends, his star descends. For this reason, the text says, "The poor person *with you*." What need is there to say, "with you"? To indicate that you are the reason that he is poor. And if you do not give to him, what will God do? God will rotate the universe in such a way that the star that is on top will sink to the bottom, and the star that is on the bottom will rise to the top.

Questions for Discussion

1. How would you characterize the biblical recommendation concerning the relationship between the wealthy and the poor?

2. There is a stark contrast, within the biblical text, between verse 4 of this text, "There shall be no poor among you," and verse 11, "The poor shall never cease." How would you explain this contradiction?

3. How do the attitudes toward the poor in the biblical text compare with the attitudes toward the poor in our own society? How do your own feelings about wealth and poverty compare with the ideas expressed in this text?

4. How do the three commentators featured earlier describe the relationship between the wealthy and the poor? Do you agree with these characterizations? Why or why not?

Biographies and Background Information

Don Isaac Abravanel (Portugal/Spain, 1437–1508) was a statesman in Portugal and then in Spain before fleeing to Italy after the expulsion of the Jews from Spain. His biblical commentary is written in the style of philosophical works of his time: he sets out a series of "questions" and then explores these through the course of the commentary.

Moshe Alshich (Turkey/Tzfat, 1508–93) was a member of the mystical circle of sixteenth-century Tzfat. His biblical commentary is homiletic in nature.

Isaac Caro (Spain/Turkey, mid-fifteenth to mid-sixteenth century) was a philosopher and biblical commentator whose biblical interpretations mix mystical, literary, and homiletic elements. Caro adopted his more famous nephew, Joseph Caro (author of the *Shulchan Arukh*), after the death of the younger Caro's father.

Discussion Questions for Chapter 1— A Vision of Economic Justice

1. How does Rabbi Jacobs describe the ideal economic situation, according to Jewish text? Do you agree with this vision? Why or why not?

2. Rabbi Jacobs lays out seven key principles for economic justice. Where do you see our own society following these principles? Where do you see our society falling short of these principles?

3. What would need to change in our own society in order to achieve the Jewish vision of economic justice? How could you imagine making these changes?

Essential Terms: Tikkun Olam, Tzedek, and Prophetic Judaism

Goal

- Participants will develop an in-depth understanding of the concept of *tikkun olam*, and will determine how to understand this term in relation to their own lives.

Trigger Exercise

1. Ask participants how many of them have heard the term *tikkun olam*. Most hands will probably go up. If there are people who have not heard the term before, ask one or two participants to offer working definitions. (You should hold off on discussing these definitions until later.)

2. Comment that some people absolutely love the term *tikkun olam*, while other people absolutely hate it. Designate one side of the room as "love" and the other as "hate." Ask participants to place themselves somewhere on this continuum between "love" and "hate," according to their own reactions to the term.

3. Ask a few participants to explain why they placed themselves where they did. What do they love or hate about *tikkun olam*?

4. Tell participants that you are going to examine some texts that discuss the development of *tikkun olam*, and will then talk again about how we understand this term today.

Text Study

Note: the terms *tikkun olam* and the verb form *l'taken olam* have not been translated here in order to encourage participants to try out their own definitions.

1. The *Aleinu* prayer

עַל כֵּן נְקַוֶּה לְךָ ה׳ אֱלֹהֵינוּ לִרְאוֹת מְהֵרָה בְּתִפְאֶרֶת עֻזֶּךָ לְהַעֲבִיר גִּלּוּלִים מִן הָאָרֶץ
וְהָאֱלִילִים כָּרוֹת יִכָּרֵתוּן. לְתַקֵּן עוֹלָם בְּמַלְכוּת שַׁדַּי וְכָל בְּנֵי בָשָׂר יִקְרְאוּ בִשְׁמֶךָ
לְהַפְנוֹת אֵלֶיךָ כָּל רִשְׁעֵי אָרֶץ. יַכִּירוּ וְיֵדְעוּ כָּל יוֹשְׁבֵי תֵבֵל כִּי לְךָ תִּכְרַע כָּל בֶּרֶךְ
תִּשָּׁבַע כָּל לָשׁוֹן. לְפָנֶיךָ ה׳ אֱלֹהֵינוּ יִכְרְעוּ וְיִפֹּלוּ. וְלִכְבוֹד שִׁמְךָ יְקָר יִתֵּנוּ. וִיקַבְּלוּ
כֻלָּם אֶת עוֹל מַלְכוּתֶךָ. וְתִמְלֹךְ עֲלֵיהֶם מְהֵרָה לְעוֹלָם וָעֶד. כִּי הַמַּלְכוּת שֶׁלְּךָ הִיא.
וּלְעוֹלְמֵי עַד תִּמְלֹךְ בְּכָבוֹד.

And so we hope in you, Adonai our God, soon to see your splendor, sweeping idolatry away so that false gods will be utterly destroyed, *l'taken olam* in your sovereignty so that all humanity will invoke your name, bringing all the earth's wicked back to you, repentant. Then, all who live will know that to you, every knee must bend, every tongue pledge loyalty. To you, Adonai, may all bow in worship, may they give honor to your glory. May everyone accept the yoke of your sovereignty. Reign over all soon and for all time. Sovereignty is yours in glory, now and forever.

2. *B'reishit Rabbah* 4:7

וַיַּעַשׂ אֱלֹהִים אֶת הָרָקִיעַ. . .לָמָּה אֵין כָּתוּב בַּשֵּׁנִי כִּי טוֹב. . .ר׳ יוֹחָנָן וְתָנֵי לָהּ בְּשֵׁם
ר׳ יוֹסֵי בַּר׳ חֲלַפְתָּא שֶׁבּוֹ נִבְרֵאת גֵּיהִנָּם כִּי עָרוּךְ מֵאֶתְמוּל תָּפְתֶּה (ישעיה ל לג)
יוֹם שֵׁשׁ בּוֹ אֶתְמוֹל וְאֵין בּוֹ שִׁלְשׁוֹם, ר׳ חֲנִינָא אָמַר שֶׁבּוֹ נִבְרֵאת מַחֲלוֹקֶת וִיהִי
מַבְדִּיל בֵּין מַיִם לְמַיִם, אָמַר ר׳ טַבְיוֹמִי אִם מַחֲלוֹקֶת שֶׁהִיא לְתִיקּוּן הָעוֹלָם
וּלְיִישׁוּבוֹ אֵין כְּתִ׳ בָּהּ כִּי טוֹב, מַחֲלוֹקֶת שֶׁהִיא לְעִרְבּוּבוֹ עַל אַחַת כַּמָּה וְכַמָּה!

"And God made the expanse, and it separated the water that was below the expanse from the water that was above the expanse. And it was so. God called the expanse 'sky.' And there was evening and there was morning, a second day" (Genesis 1:7–8). Why is it that "it was good" is not written in connection with the second day?... Rabbi Chanina said, "Because on that day, a schism was created, as it is written, 'let it divide the waters.'" R. Tavyomi said, "If because of a division made *l'taken olam* and to stabilize it, 'it was good' is not written in connection with that day, how much more so should this apply to a schism that leads to the confusion of the world!?!"

3. Mishnah, *Gittin* 4:2

בראשונה היה עושה בית דין במקום אחר ומבטלו התקין רבן גמליאל הזקן
שלא יהו עושין כן מפני תקון העולם בראשונה היה משנה שמו ושמה שם עירו
ושם עירה והתקין רבן גמליאל הזקן שיהא איש פלוני וכל שם שיש לו
אשה פלונית וכל שום שיש לה מפני תקון העולם:

At first, a husband would bring a court wherever he was and annul the *get* (if he changed his mind after sending a *get* to his wife). Rabban Gamaliel the Elder established (*hitkin*) that this should not be done, for the sake of *tikkun olam*. At first, the husband could change his name, or his wife's name, or the name of his town or of his wife's town (meaning—he could write the *get* using a nickname for himself, his wife, or their town). Rabban Gamaliel the Elder established that for the sake of *tikkun olam*, he should write: "The man so-and-so" and any name that he has; "the woman so-and-so" and any name that she has.

4. Mishnah, *Gittin* 4:5

מי שחציו עבד וחציו בן חורין עובד את רבו יום אחד ואת עצמו יום אחד דברי
בית הלל אמרו לו בית שמאי את תקנתם את רבו ואת עצמו לא תקנתם לישא שפחה
אי אפשר שכבר חציו בן חורין בת חורין אי אפשר שכבר חציו עבד יבטל והלא
לא נברא העולם אלא לפריה ורביה שנאמר (ישעיה מ"ה) לא תהו בראה לשבת
יצרה אלא מפני תקון העולם כופין את רבו ועושה אותו בן חורין וכותב שטר
על חצי דמיו וחזרו בית הלל להורות כדברי בית שמאי:

Beit Hillel said, "One who is half slave and half free works for his master one day and for himself the other day." Beit Shammai said, "You have set things right for the master but you have not set things right for the slave. He cannot marry a female slave because he is already half free, and he cannot marry a free woman because he is half a slave. Shall he then desist [from having children]? But wasn't the world only made to be populated, as it says, 'God did not create it as a waste; God formed it to be inhabited' (Isaiah 45:18)? Rather for the sake of *tikkun olam*, we compel his master to emancipate him and the slave writes an IOU for half his purchase price." Beit Hillel retracted [their opinion and] ruled like Beit Shammai.

5. Mishnah, *Gittin* 4:6

אין פודין את השבויים יותר על כדי דמיהן מפני תקון העולם ואין מבריחין את
השבויין מפני תקון העולם רבן שמעון בן גמליאל אומר מפני תקנת השבויין
ואין לוקחים ספרים תפילין ומזוזות מן הגוים יותר על כדי דמיהן מפני תקון
העולם:

Captives should not be redeemed for more than their value, for the sake of *tikkun olam*. Captives should not be helped to escape, for the sake of *tikkun olam*. Rabban Shimon ben Gamaliel says [that the reason is] to prevent the ill-treatment of fellow captives. Torah scrolls, *tefillin*, and *mezuzot* are not bought from Gentiles at more than their value, for the sake of *tikkun olam*.

6. Lawrence Fine, *Physician of the Soul, Healer of the Cosmos: Isaac Luria and His Kabbalistic Fellowship*, 141–144

In Lurianic thinking, then, the original crisis that occurred within the realm of the divine was not dependent on the misdeeds of humanity but had to do with qualities of being and dynamic processes intrinsic to divinity itself. Human beings, however, exacerbated the crisis and thus have an indispensable role to play in the completion of the work of cosmic mending....

In Luria's view, then, the most fundamental and ultimate goal of human existence is *tiqqun*. The project of *tiqqun*, the liberation of divine light in all of its forms from its entrapment in the material sphere, its return to its source on high, and the ascent of all the worlds to their proper place within the structure of the cosmos, required the most elaborate and painstaking regimen of contemplative devotion. The ritual practices that Isaac Luria taught his disciples were intended to accomplish nothing less than repair of the defects engendered by the primordial processes of divine emanation and by the primal transgression of humankind. Such reparation ... was conceived of by Luria and his circle as synonymous with messianic redemption.

7. Antonio Villaraigosa (mayor of Los Angeles), address to Union for Reform Judaism Biennial, 2007

There is a central idea that justice and opportunity exists for none of us if it fails to reach all of us. And there is the faith that our best days are yet to come.
I may have been Catholic, born and raised. But the lessons of my life, and a career in public service, have always found their clearest articulation in Hebrew: *Tikkun Olam*, *Tzedakah*, and *Mitzvot*.

8. Website of Wilshire Boulevard Temple

TIKKUN OLAM—Repairing the World—is the Jewish mandate to give more than we take. We care for the stranger, the widow and those in need through direct social action and multifaceted encounters with other faith traditions.

In Torah we read, *Tzedek, tzedek tirdof*—Righteousness, righteousness must you pursue! We respond to that *mitzvah* in many ways as we address the various imbalances in the world.

9. Anthony Ramirez, "Congestion Pricing, Asthma and Tikkun Olam," *New York Times*, April 7, 2007

Mr. (Michael) Bloomberg told a conference of ministers at the Bethel A.M.E. Church on West 132nd Street in Harlem that his administration was committed to removing "disease-causing soot" from the city's air....

"In my faith, the Jewish faith," Mr. Bloomberg continued, "there is a religious obligation called *tikkun olam*, or to make the world whole, or to correct error and end injustice. And that responsibility is found among people of good will in every faith."

Questions for Discussion

1. Before you looked at these texts, how would you have translated or explained the term *tikkun olam*?
2. How would you translate the term *tikkun olam* or *l'taken olam* in each of these texts? Pretend that you have never heard the term before, and base your translations only on context clues.
3. Which of the definitions of *tikkun olam* presented in these texts do you find most compelling? Are there any that you find problematic? Are there any definitions that surprised you?
4. Now that you have studied these texts, has your understanding of the term *tikkun olam* changed at all? How or how not? Are you more or less inclined to use this term in your own life and work? Would you at all shift where you stood on the love-hate continuum with which we started this discussion?

Biographies and Background Information

The **Aleinu prayer**, now recited at the end of every Jewish prayer service, may have been written as early as the first century CE. This prayer acknowledges responsibility for worshiping and exalting God, and looks forward to a time when God's reign will fill the entire world.

B'reishit Rabbah (fifth century CE) is one of the earliest compilations of *midrash* (rabbinic interpretations of and expansions on the biblical stories). *B'reishit Rabbah* includes narratives and interpretive texts based on the book of Genesis.

The **Mishnah** is the first layer of the Talmud. Codified around 200 CE, the Mishnah includes basic case law with minimal explanation or expansion. The Mishnah is divided into six sections, or *sedarim*, each of which focuses primarily on one area of law.

A **get** is a Jewish divorce document. According to traditional Jewish law, a man unilaterally divorces his wife by presenting her with a *get*. (Contemporary Jewish legal authorities have developed a number of means to ensure that a woman who wishes to initiate a divorce is able to do so as well.) As soon as the wife receives the *get*, she is divorced and free to remarry. The texts presented here consider cases in which a woman might have doubts about whether the *get* she has received is valid, and therefore whether she may remarry.

Isaac Luria was the leader of a group of sixteenth-century mystics in Tzfat, now part of northern Israel.

Discussion Questions for Chapter 2—
Essential Terms: Tikkun Olam, Tzedek, *and Prophetic Judaism*

1. This chapter introduces three terms—*tikkun olam, tzedek,* and prophetic Judaism, all of which are often used to describe social justice work. Have you ever used one or more of these terms to describe work that you were doing? In what context? Which of these terms do you find most compelling and why?

2. If you were already familiar with any or all of these terms before reading this chapter, has your understanding of any of these terms changed? In what ways? Do you feel more or less compelled to use any of these terms to describe work that you or your community are doing? Why?

3. Rabbi Jacobs asserts that "in some circles, *tikkun olam, tzedek,* and 'prophetic Judaism' have become overused to the point of losing any real meaning." Do you agree? Why or why not? What is the value of finding more precise definitions of these terms?

Defining Poverty and the Poor

Goal

- Participants will be able to offer a Jewish definition of poverty.

Trigger Exercise

1. Give each participant a few index cards.
2. Ask each participant to write, on each index card, one way that s/he would finish the following sentence: When I think about the poor, what comes to mind is_____. Participants may use as many or as few cards as they wish. Encourage participants to be as honest as possible and let them know that nobody will know what they wrote.
3. Collect all of the index cards in a hat or box and mix them up.
4. Pass the hat around and have each participant, in turn, choose one card and read what is on it.
5. When the group has read all of the cards, ask the group what reactions they had to hearing these associations. What trends did they notice? What surprised them? What emotions came to mind when they heard these associations?

Text Study

1. Exodus 22:21–26

כא כָּל-אַלְמָנָה וְיָתוֹם, לֹא תְעַנּוּן. כב אִם-עַנֵּה תְעַנֶּה, אֹתוֹ כִּי אִם-צָעֹק יִצְעַק
אֵלַי, שָׁמֹעַ אֶשְׁמַע צַעֲקָתוֹ. כג וְחָרָה אַפִּי, וְהָרַגְתִּי אֶתְכֶם בֶּחָרֶב; וְהָיוּ נְשֵׁיכֶם
אַלְמָנוֹת, וּבְנֵיכֶם יְתֹמִים.

כד אִם-כֶּסֶף תַּלְוֶה אֶת-עַמִּי, אֶת-הֶעָנִי עִמָּךְ לֹא-תִהְיֶה לוֹ, כְּנֹשֶׁה; לֹא-תְשִׂימוּן
עָלָיו, נֶשֶׁךְ. כה אִם-חָבֹל תַּחְבֹּל, שַׂלְמַת רֵעֶךָ עַד-בֹּא הַשֶּׁמֶשׁ, תְּשִׁיבֶנּוּ לוֹ. כו כִּי
הוּא כְסוּתֹה לְבַדָּהּ, הוּא שִׂמְלָתוֹ לְעֹרוֹ; בַּמֶּה יִשְׁכָּב וְהָיָה כִּי-יִצְעַק אֵלַי, וְשָׁמַעְתִּי
כִּי-חַנּוּן אָנִי.

You shall not ill-treat any widow or orphan. If you do mistreat them, I will heed their outcry as soon as they cry out to Me, and My anger shall blaze forth and I will put you to the sword, and your own wives shall become widows and your children orphans. If you lend money to My people, to the poor among you, do not act toward them as a creditor; exact no interest from them. If you take your neighbor's garment in pledge, you must return it to him before the sun sets; it is his only clothing, the sole covering for his skin. In what else shall he sleep? Therefore, if he cries out to Me, I will pay heed, for I am compassionate.

2. Babylonian Talmud, *Ketubot* 67b

תנו רבנן די מחסורו אתה מצווה עליו לפרנסו ואי אתה מצווה עליו לעשרו אשר
יחסר לו אפילו סוס לרכוב עליו ועבד לרוץ לפניו אמרו עליו על הלל הזקן
שלקח לעני בן טובים אחד סוס לרכוב עליו ועבד לרוץ לפניו פעם אחת לא
מצא עבד לרוץ לפניו ורץ לפניו שלשה מילין.

Our Rabbis taught: "Sufficient for [the poor person's] needs" means that you are commanded to maintain this person, but you are not commanded to make this person rich. "What the poor person is lacking" [includes] even a horse to ride upon and a slave to run before him. It was related about Hillel the Elder that he bought a certain poor man of a good family a horse to ride upon and a slave to run before him. On one occasion he could not find a slave to run before him, so he himself ran before him for three miles.

3. *Sh'mot Rabbah* 31:12

אמר לו הקב"ה :מה אתה רוצה עניות, או יסורין ? אמר לו איוב : רבון העולם!
מקבל אני עלי כל יסורין שבעולם ולא עניות, כשאצא לשוק ואין בידי פרוטה
לקנות מה אוכל . . .לכך קשה עניות מכל היסורין. לכך נאמר :**את העני עמך**.
אמר הקב"ה : לא דיו ענייתו, אלא שאתה נוטל הימנו רבית?

God said to Job, "Which would you prefer—poverty or suffering?" Job responded, "Master of
the universe—I will take all of the sufferings in the world as long as I don't become poor, for
if I go to the marketplace and don't have any money to buy food, what will I eat?"... This
shows us that poverty is worse than all of the other sufferings in the world. For this reason,
the Torah says, "If you lend money to one of my people, to the poor among you … you shall
not charge interest" (Exodus 22:25). God says, "His poverty was not enough for him? Do you
also have to take interest from him?!?"

4. Babylonian Talmud, *Ketubot* 67b

רבי חנינא הוה ההוא עניא דהוה רגיל לשדורי ליה ארבעה זוזי כל מעלי שבתא
יומא חד שדרינהו ניהליה ביד דביתהו אתאי אמרה ליה לא צריך מאי חזית
שמעי דהוה קאמרי ליה במה אתה סועד ?

גמרא בטלי כסף או בטלי זהב אמר היינו דאמר רבי אלעזר בואו ונחזיק טובה
לרמאין שאלמלא הן היינו חוטאין בכל יום שנאמר (דברים טו) ו(קרא עליך אל
ה' והיה בך חטא.

Rabbi Chanina had a poor man to whom he regularly sent four *zuz* [a sum of money] every
Friday afternoon. One day, he sent that sum through his wife, who came back and told him
that [the man] didn't need it. "What did you see?" [Rabbi Chanina asked.] "I heard him being
asked, 'With what will you dine? With the silver settings or the gold ones?'" He said, "This is
what Rabbi Eliezer meant when he said, 'Come, let us be grateful to the cheaters, for if not for
them, we would be sinning every day, as it is said, "And [the poor person] cries unto God
against you, and it will be a sin on you" (Deuteronomy 15:9).'

5. *Vayikra Rabbah* 34:4

אמר העשיר לאותו העני : לית את אזיל לעי ונגיס?? חמי שקיין, חמי כרעין,
חמי כרסוון, חמי קפרן .א"ל הקדוש ברוך הוא : לא דייך שלא נתת לו משלך
מאומה, אלא במה שנתתי לו אתה מכניס לו עין רעה ?!

If the rich man says to this same poor man, "Why do you not go and work and get food? Look at those hips! Look at those legs! Look at that fat body! Look at those lumps of flesh!" I, the Blessed Holy One say to him, "Is it not enough that you have not given him anything of yours, but you must set the evil eye upon what I have given him?"

6. Rabbi Moshe Feinstein, *Igg'rot Moshe, Yoreh De'ah* 4:37

ואף כשהוא עצמו גרם לזה שלא בשביל לימוד תורה, והוא פושע, חייבין
לפרנסו מצדקה . . . מי שהתעצל לעבוד את שדותיו אף שהוא בשביל עצלות,
ומכרם ואכל את דמיהן ונעשה עני . . . נוטל לקט שכחה ופאה, וגם צריכין ליתן
לו מקופה של צדקה.

Even if he caused himself [to lose all of his property] not for the sake of studying Torah, though he is a sinner, we are obligated to give him *tzedakah* [monetary or other material support] ... one who refrains from working his fields, even out of laziness, and sells them and consumes the profits and becomes poor may collect *leket, shikh'cha* and *pe'ah* [certain types of agricultural *tzedakah*]; we are also obligated to give to this person from the communal *tzedakah* fund.

Questions for Discussion

1. How do these texts describe the experience of poverty? How do these descriptions correspond with the poverty that you personally have witnessed or heard about?
2. According to these texts, what should be the relationship between the wealthy and the poor? Do you agree? Why or why not?
3. A number of these texts take up the question of whether there is such a thing as the "undeserving poor." Have you heard this term before? In what context? How do these texts address this question? Do you agree or disagree with this approach?

Biographies and Background Information

The **Talmud** is the Jewish oral law. It consists of two parts: the Mishnah (codified by 200 CE), which consists primarily of concise legal statements; and the Gemara (codified around the sixth century CE), which expands upon and comments on the Mishnah. The Talmud is divided into tractates (Hebrew: *masekhtot*), each of which deals primarily with a certain set of topics.

Sh'mot Rabbah is a collection of *midrashim* (stories, interpretations, and expansions) on the book of Exodus. The work, probably composed in the medieval period, is divided into two sections. The first section consists of a line-by-line commentary on the beginning of the book of Exodus. The second section contains a series of homilies on the latter part of the book.

Vayikra Rabbah is a collection of *midrash* that consists of homilies on the book of Leviticus. It was probably compiled around the fifth century CE, and therefore is one of the earliest collections of *midrash*.

Rabbi Moshe Feinstein (1895–1986) was one of the most significant American Orthodox rabbis of the twentieth century. He wrote a number of influential *teshuvot* (legal opinions) on subjects including unionization, smoking, and medical ethics.

Discussion Questions for Chapter 3— Defining Poverty and the Poor

1. How would you define poverty? Does your definition correspond to the definitions laid out in this chapter? How are the definitions similar and different?
2. Rabbi Jacobs notes that traditional sources often speak about poverty through the medium of stories. What stories have you read or heard that effectively conveyed the experience of poverty? What role do you think storytelling has, or should have, in combating poverty?
3. Some of the sources cited in this chapter suggest that "what goes around comes around"—that is, the wealthy have a personal self-interest in supporting the poor. Do you agree? Why or why not?

Sufficient for One's Needs:
The Collection and Allocation of Tzedakah

Goals

- Participants will understand some of the factors that may influence decisions about where to give *tzedakah*.
- Participants will examine their own giving history and goals in light of Jewish concepts of *tzedakah*.

Trigger Exercise

1. Ask participants to write down one question they have about their own giving. These questions can address any aspect of giving, including issues of how much to give, where to give, how to give, and other concerns.
2. Go around the room and ask each participant to tell the group his or her question. Write these on the board or on a flip chart.
3. Divide the participants into pairs or into groups of three or four. Assign each small group two to three of the questions that participants have generated. Give each small group the included texts, and ask them to read these texts together, and to try to formulate responses to their assigned questions, based on these texts.
4. Bring all the participants back together, and ask each small group to share one insight they learned from the texts they studied, and/or one question that remains for them.

Text Study

1. Maimonides, *Mishneh Torah*, *Matanot l'Aniyim* (Gifts to the Poor) 7:1–2

א מצות עשה ליתן צדקה לעניי ישראל כפי מה שראוי לעני, אם היתה יד
הנותן משגת שנאמר פתוח תפתח את ידך, לו (דברים טו,ח)ונאמר והחזקת
בו, גר ותושב וחי עימך (ויקרא כה,לה) ונאמר וחי אחיך, עימך(ויקרא
כה,לו) .[ב] וכל הרואה עני מבקש, והעלים עיניו ממנו, ולא נתן לו צדקה עובר
בלא תעשה, שנאמר "לא תאמץ את לבבך, ולא תקפוץ את ידך, מאחיך,
האביון (דברים טו,ז.)

It is a positive commandment to give *tzedakah* to the poor, according to what is fitting for that
poor person, if one can afford to do so.... And anyone who sees a poor person begging and
averts one's eyes from this person and does not give him/her *tzedakah* has violated a negative
commandment, as it says, "Do not harden your heart and do not close your hand to your poor
brother" (Deuteronomy 15:7).

2. *Shulchan Arukh*, *Yoreh De'ah* 249:1

שיעור נתינתה, אם ידו משגת יתן כפי צורך העניים. ואם אין ידו משגת כל כך,
יתן עד חומש נכסיו, מצוה מן המובחר ;ואחד מעשרה, מדה בינונית ; פחות
מכאן, עין רעה .וחומש זה שאמרו, שנה ראשונה מהקרן, מכאן ואילך חומש
שהרויח בכל שנה.

The amount that one should give: If you can afford to do so, you should give according to the
needs of the poor. And if you can't afford this much, you should give up to one-fifth of one's
property—this is the ideal fulfillment of the *mitzvah*. And one-tenth is the ordinary way. Anything less than this is associated with the evil eye. In regard to the one-fifth—in the first year,
one should give this from one's capital; after this, one should give from one's profit.

3. Babylonian Talmud, *Bava Metzia* 71a

דתני רב יוסף : (שמות כ"ב) אם כסף תלוה את עמי את העני עמך, עמי ונכרי -
עמי קודם, עני ועשיר - עני קודם, ענייך ועניי עירך - ענייך קודמין, עניי עירך
ועניי עיר אחרת - עניי עירך קודמין.

Rabbi Yosef taught [the meaning of the verse], "If you lend money to my people, to the poor
among you, do not act as a creditor toward them" (Exodus 22:24). In the case of a Jew and a
non-Jew, the Jew takes precedence; a poor person and a wealthy person, the poor person

takes precedence; a poor person from your family and one not from your family, your family takes precedence; a poor person of your own city and a poor person of another city, the poor of your city take precedence.

4. Babylonian Talmud, *Gittin* 61a

אין ממחין ביד עניי נכרים בלקט בשכחה ובפאה, מפני דרכי שלום. ת״ר: מפרנסים עניי נכרים עם עניי ישראל, ומבקרין חולי נכרים עם חולי ישראל, וקוברין מתי נכרים עם מתי ישראל, מפני דרכי שלום.

The Rabbis taught: We sustain the non-Jewish poor along with the Jewish poor and visit the non-Jewish sick along with the Jewish sick, and bury the non-Jewish dead along with the Jewish dead for the sake of peace (*mipnei darkhei shalom*).

5. *Beit Yosef, Yoreh De'ah* 257:9–10

ט וכתב עוד שם (סי׳ תקב) פרק הדר (עירובין סג.) אמר רב כהנא כל הנותן מתנותיו לכהן אחד מביא אף לעולם מכאן שלא יתן אדם כל צדקותיו לקרובו אחד ולהניח שאר קרובים גם לא לאדם אחד ולא לשאר בני אדם.

י וכתב עוד שם המחלק צדקה צריך ליזהר שלא ירבה לקרובו יותר משאר בני אדם כההיא דפרק כל כתבי (שבת קיח:) דאמר רבי יוסי יהא חלקי מגבאי צדקה ולא ממחלקי צדקה ופירש רש״י שהמחלק מרבה לקרוביו וגוזל שאר עניים.

The Mordechai (commentary on the Talmud) wrote: [the Talmud, in tractate *Eruvin* 63a, says] Rav Kahana said, "Anyone who gives all of his gifts to a single *kohen* (member of the priestly clan) brings anger to the world." From this, we learn that one should not give all of one's *tzedakah* to a single relative, abandoning all other relatives, nor should one give all of one's *tzedakah* to a single person and not to anyone else.

He also wrote that one who doles out *tzedakah* must be careful not to give more to one's relatives than to anyone else. Similarly, elsewhere in the Talmud (tractate *Shabbat* 118b), Rabbi Yosi said, "May I be among the collectors of *tzedakah* and not among those charged with distributing it." Rashi explained, one who distributes *tzedakah* is likely to give more to one's relatives and thereby to steal from the rest of the poor.

6. Rabbi Moshe Sofer, *She'elot and Teshuvot of the Chatam Sofer* 2:231

כי יהיה בך אביון באחד שעריך דדריש ספרי אביון התאב קודם ושוב
דריש עניי עמך קודמין וכו' ועניי קרוביך קודמין כ' ז"ל לכן הקדים התאב תאב
קודם לומר עניי עירך קודמין לעניי עיר אחרת היינו אם שניהם צריכים למזון או
לכסות אבל אם עניי עירך יש להם כדי חיותם אלא שאין להם הרוחה כלל לזה
עניי עיר אחרת קודמין לעניי עירך דהתאב תאב קודם.

"If there is a poor person within your gates," *Sifre* (collection of legal *midrash* on the book of Deuteronomy) expounds this verse saying, "When one is starving, the one who is starving takes precedence" and then expounds, "The poor of your city take precedence over the poor of another city." That is to say—this applies if both poor people need food or clothing. However, if the poor of your city have what they need to live, but just don't have any extra money [and the poor of the other city don't have food or clothing], then the poor of the other city take precedence over the poor of your city, for the neediest takes precedence.

7. Rabbi Eliezer Waldenburg, *She'elot and Teshuvot of Tzitz Eliezer* 9:1

וזה שמתיר במהר"ם שם לקנות מהכסף גם ספרים ללמוד בהם ולהשאילן
לאחרים, יש לומר דהוא זה גם כן מפני שישאילם לנצרכים ללמוד בהם שכל
הנצרך להם עני הוא בחסר לו זה והר"ז כמספק לו מזון רוחני שאין זה גרוע
ממספק מזון גשמי לחסר לו, אבל לעשות מצוה כזאת שהכסף לא ילך למזון
גשמי או רוחני למי שחסר לו מזה יודה שפיר גם המהר"מ שאין לעשותה בכסף
מעשר, וראי' להאמור יש להביא מדברי ספר בית דינו של שלמה חיו"ד סי' א'
שכותב דאבל לקנות ספרים לבני עניים זה ודאי דבא מן המעשר, שכ"כ הרב
שכה"ג עיי"ש. והיינו מפני שהמצאת מזון רוחני לעניים ג"כ לנתינת צדקה
תחשב וכנ"ז.

(Commenting on Rabbi Meir of Rothenberg's permission to use money designated for the poor to purchase books for study or to be lent to others:) One can say that he permits this because the books will be lent for study to those who need them, and anyone who needs these books is considered poor, insofar as this person lacks them. This is like distributing spiritual food, and is no less desirable than distributing physical food to those who need it. However, as for using this money for a *mitzvah* (such as buying candles for the synagogue)—in this case, the money does not go to either physical or spiritual food for those who need it ... and one should not use the money in this way. I have seen an opinion that ... one may certainly use this money to buy books for the children of the poor, for providing spiritual food to the poor is also considered to be *tzedakah*.

Questions for Discussion

Imagine that you have $10,000 to give in *tzedakah*. Basing your actions on the sources above, how would you distribute this money among the following groups or individuals?

1. A group organizing parents to secure a new high school in a low-income neighborhood needs $40,000 to hire an organizer.
2. A soup kitchen in your city needs $8,000 to buy enough food to feed its clients for this month.
3. A Washington, D.C., advocacy organization that focuses on economic justice issues needs $10,000 to create a Web-based advocacy center.
4. Your first cousin, who recently lost her job and is struggling to support herself, needs $1,500 to cover rent and other expenses this month.
5. An organization that involves volunteers in building affordable housing units needs $25,000 to hire a part-time volunteer coordinator.
6. An organization that is running health clinics in Africa needs $15,000 to buy medicine for the next six months.
7. A Jewish group that involves Jews in local economic justice issues needs $20,000 for a part-time organizer who will involve individual Jews in a campaign to secure higher wages for workers in a local kosher food plant.
8. A local Jewish nursing home needs $40,000 for emergency repairs on its roof.
9. An organization that supports hospitals in Israel needs $50,000 to buy a new ambulance.
10. A synagogue whose members are active in volunteering and in local political issues needs $5,000 to provide political training for its congregants.
11. An organization that offers English language instruction, GED tutoring, and job training needs $5,000 to buy new textbooks.
12. A legal clinic needs $10,000 to hire a law student to do research on a case that may result in the back payment of $1 million in wages to low-income workers.
13. A community bank that gives small loans to people who want to start their own businesses needs $30,000 to start a job training program.
14. A group that is planning a rally at the mall in support of a national health care system needs $15,000 to rent buses.
15. A man begging for money on your street needs $300 to stay at an SRO (single room occupancy hotel) this month.

Biographies and Background Information

The **Talmud** is the Jewish oral law. It consists of two parts: the Mishnah (codified by 200 CE), which consists primarily of concise legal statements; and the Gemara (codified around the sixth century CE), which expands upon and comments on the Mishnah. The Talmud is divided into tractates (Hebrew: *masekhtot*), each of which deals primarily with a certain set of topics.

Rabbi Moshe Sofer (1762–1839) was a German rabbi often called by the name of his most famous book, the *Chatam Sofer*. He is best known for his opposition to the German Reform movement and to all forms of innovation in Judaism.

Rabbi Eliezer Waldenburg (Jerusalem, 1917–2006) was a leading figure in the Israeli rabbinate. He is best known for his writings on medical ethics, and for taking courageous and often progressive positions on issues such as transsexuality and economics.

Maimonides (a.k.a. Rambam, Cordoba/Egypt, 1135–1204) is one of the best-known figures in Jewish philosophy and law. His major works include the *Mishneh Torah*, a restatement of Talmudic law aimed at ordinary Jews, and *Moreh Nevuchim*, a philosophical work in which he grapples with the major philosophical questions of the scholarly Arabic world of his day through a Jewish lens.

The **Shulchan Arukh** and the **Beit Yosef** were both written by Rabbi Joseph Caro (Israel, 1488–1575). The *Shulchan Arukh* is probably the most authoritative code of Jewish law. The *Beit Yosef* is a commentary on an earlier code of Jewish law, and forms the basis for the *Shulchan Arukh*.

Discussion Questions for Chapter 4— Sufficient for One's Needs: The Collection and Allocation of Tzedakah

1. How often do you give *tzedakah*? How do you make decisions about how much money to give away? How do you make decisions about which individuals receive your *tzedakah* money?
2. Rabbi Jacobs distinguishes between *tzedakah*, which connotes gifts to the poor, and philanthropy, which does not necessarily benefit the poor. Do you agree with this distinction? Within your own giving, which gifts would you characterize as *tzedakah* and which would you characterize as philanthropy?
3. Have you experienced any personal spiritual benefits from giving *tzedakah*? How would you describe this feeling? How would you imagine making *tzedakah* a central part of your own spiritual practice?
4. Rabbi Jacobs distinguishes between the *tzedakah* obligations of the individual and those of the government. Do you agree with this distinction? Why or why not?

5

Servants to Servants or Servants to God: Workers, Employers, and Unions

Goal

- Participants will develop an understanding of some Jewish approaches to the relationship between employers and employees.

Trigger Exercise

1. Divide participants into pairs.
2. Ask each pair to discuss what was the most positive workplace situation they have ever experienced? What was the most negative?
3. What factors contributed to their positive or negative feelings about each of these workplace situations?
4. Bring the group back together, and ask participants to share any insights that they gained from their conversation. Did they see any common themes in their own and their partner's story? Did they learn anything new about what makes a positive or negative workplace?

Text Study

Note that Jewish text distinguishes between two classes of workers: the *po'el*, who does unskilled work and is paid by the day; and the *kablan*, an artisan who does contract work and is paid by the product. The texts below deal with the *po'el*, who is most similar to today's low-wage workers, who are paid by the hour.

1. Deuteronomy 24:14–15

יד לֹא-תַעֲשֹׁק שָׂכִיר, עָנִי וְאֶבְיוֹן, מֵאַחֶיךָ, אוֹ מִגֵּרְךָ אֲשֶׁר בְּאַרְצְךָ בִּשְׁעָרֶיךָ. טו
בְּיוֹמוֹ תִתֵּן שְׂכָרוֹ וְלֹא-תָבוֹא עָלָיו הַשֶּׁמֶשׁ, כִּי עָנִי הוּא, וְאֵלָיו, הוּא נֹשֵׂא אֶת-
נַפְשׁוֹ; וְלֹא-יִקְרָא עָלֶיךָ אֶל-יְהוָה, וְהָיָה בְךָ חֵטְא.

Do not oppress the hired laborer who is poor and needy, whether he is one of your people or one of the sojourners in your land within your gates. Give him his wages in the daytime, and do not let the sun set on them, for he is poor, and his life depends on them, lest he cry out to God about you, for this will be counted as a sin for you.

2. Babylonian Talmud, *Bava Metzia* 112a

מפני מה עלה זה בכבש ונתלה באילן ומסר את עצמו למיתה לא על שכרו דבר
אחר ואליו הוא נושא את נפשו כל הכובש שכר שכיר כאילו נוטל נפשו ממנו.

Why does he climb a ladder or hang from a tree or risk death? Is it not for his wages? Another interpretation—"His life depends on them" indicates that a person who denies a hired laborer his wages is considered to have taken his life from him.

3. Jonah Gerondi, *Sefer haYirah* (Spain, d. 1263)

השמר מלצער בע"ח הן בהמה הן עוף, וכ"ש שלא לצער אדם שהוא עשוי
בצלם המקום. אם אתה רוצה לשכור פועלים ומצאת עניים יהיו עניים בני ביתך,
ואך אל תבזה אותם, אך דרך כבוד תצוה להם, ותשלם שכרם משלם.

Be careful not to afflict a living creature, whether animal or fowl, and even more so not to afflict a human being, who is created in God's image. If you want to hire workers and you find that they are poor, they should become like poor members of your household. You should not disgrace them, for you shall command them respectfully, and should pay their salaries.

4. Rabbi Moshe ben Nachman (Ramban/Nachmanides, Spain, 1194–1270) on Deuteronomy 24:14

כי עני הוא - כרובי הנשכרים, ואל השכר הזה הוא נושא נפשו שיקנה בו מזון
להחיות נפשו... הכוונה בו שתפרענו ביומו, שאם לא תפרענו בצאתו ממלאכתו
מיד הנה ילך לביתו וישאר שכרו אתך עד בקר וימות הוא ברעב בלילה.

For he is poor—like the majority of hired laborers, and he depends on the wages to buy food by which to live ... if he does not collect the wages right away as he is leaving work, he will go home, and his wages will remain with you until the morning, and he will die of hunger that night.

5. Mishnah, *Bava Metzia* 7:1

השוכר את הפועלים, ואמר להם להשכים ולהעריב—מקום שנהגו שלא להשכים
ושלא להעריב, אינו יכול לכופן ; מקום שנהגו לזון, יזון ; לספק במתיקה,
יספק :הכול כמנהג המדינה. מעשה ברבי יוחנן בן מתיה שאמר לבנו, צא
ושכור לנו פועלים, ופסק עימהם מזונות. וכשבא אצל אביו, אמר לו, אפילו את
עושה להם כסעודת שלמה בשעתה, לא יצאת ידי חובתך, שהם בני אברהם
יצחק ויעקוב ; אלא עד שלא יתחילו במלאכה, צא ואמור להם, על מנת שאין
לכם אלא פת וקטנית בלבד. רבן שמעון בן גמליאל אומר, לא היה צריך לומר,
אלא הכול כמנהג המדינה.

One who hires workers and instructs them to begin work early and to stay late—in a place in which it is not the custom to begin work early and to stay late, the employer may not force them to do so. In a place in which it is the custom to feed the workers, he must do so. In a place in which it is the custom to distribute sweets, he must do so. Everything goes according to the custom of the land [*minhag hamakom*].

A story about Rabbi Yochanan ben Matya, who told his son, "Go, hire us workers." His son went and promised them food (without specifying what kind, or how much). When he returned, his father said to him, "My son! Even if you gave them a feast like that of King Solomon, you would not have fulfilled your obligation toward them, for they are the children of Abraham, Isaac and Jacob. However, as they have not yet begun to work, go back and say to them that their employment is conditional on their not demanding more than bread and vegetables." Rabbi Shimon ben Gamliel said, "It is not necessary to make such a stipulation. Everything goes according to the custom of the place."

6. Babylonian Talmud, *Bava Metzia* 83a

פשיטא לא צריכא דטפא להו אאגרייהו מהו דתימא אמר להו האי דטפאי לכו
אאגרייכו אדעתא דמקדמיתו ומחשכיתו בהדאי קא משמע לן דאמרו ליה האי
דטפת לן אדעתא דעבדינן לך עבידתא שפירתא.

We need [the statement forbidding employers to force employees to start early or to work late] for the case in which the employer raises the workers' wages. In the case in which he says to them, "I raised your wages in order that you would begin work early and stay late," they may reply, "You raised our wages in order that we would do better work."

7. Babylonian Talmud, *Bava Batra* 8b–9a

ורשאין בני העיר להתנות על המדות ועל השערים, ועל שכר פועלים ולהסיע
על קיצתן ...הנהו בי תרי טבחי דעבדי עניינא בהדי הדדי, דכל מאן דעביד ביומא
דחבריה נקרעוה למשכיה. אזל חד מנייהו עבד ביומא דחבריה, קרעו למשכיה;
אתו לקמיה דרבא, חייבינהו רבא לשלומי. איתיביה רב יימר בר שלמיא לרבא:
ולהסיע על קיצתם ! לא אהדר ליה רבא. אמר רב פפא: שפיר עבד דלא אהדר
ליה מידי, ה״מ היכא דליכא אדם חשוב, אבל היכא דאיכא אדם חשוב - לאו כל
כמינייהו דמתנו.

The people of the city are permitted to stipulate weights and measures and to set workers'
wages and to establish penalties for breaking the rules … there were two butchers who made
an agreement with each other that if either one worked on the other's day, [the one whose
day it was] could tear up the other's hide. One of them went and worked on the other's day,
and [the one whose day it was] tore up the other's hide. They went before Rava, and Rava
compelled [the one who did the tearing] to pay compensation. Rav Yemar bar Shlamiya asked
Rava, "But it says 'they can establish penalties for breaking the rules!'" Rava did not answer
him. Rav Papa said, "Rava was right not to answer, for these words only apply when there is
no *adam h_ashuv* (important person), but in this case, when there is an *adam h_ashuv*, they cannot make a stipulation."

8. Rabbi Shlomo ben Aderet, *She'elot u'Teshuvot* 4:185

דבר ברור הוא, שהצבור רשאים לגדור ולתקן תקנות ולעשות הסכמות, כפי מה
שיראה בעיניהם, והרי הוא קיים כדין התורה. ויכולים לקנוס ולענוש כל העובר
בכל אשר יסכימו ביניהם, ובלבד שיסכימו בכך כל הציבור, באין מעכב. וכן אם
יסכימו כל בני מלאכה אחת שבעיר... כל בני חבורה אחת, הרי הם כבני עיר
אחת בפני עצמה, לכלל דברים אלו. וכן כל ציבור וציבור, רשאים לעשות
לעצמן כן, ולקנוס ולענוש שלא מדין התורה.

This is clear—the community is permitted to make rules, stipulations, and agreements
according to their own needs, and these are given the weight of Torah laws. They can enact
fines and punishments for anyone who transgresses any of the laws to which the community
has agreed, as long as the whole community has agreed to these. Similarly, all of the members
of one trade in the city [may make a binding agreement among themselves] … for members
of an organization are, unto themselves, like the people of a city in regard to these things.
Similarly, every community is permitted to make enactments for itself and to establish fines
and punishments beyond those mandated by the Torah.

Questions for Discussion

1. How do these texts describe the relationship between workers and employers? What are some of the obligations that each party has toward the other? How might some of the conditions mentioned in these texts apply to contemporary workers and employers?

2. How do you understand the concept of "the custom of the land" (*minhag hamakom*)? Can you think of any contemporary parallels to this concept? How do the texts presented here both support and challenge this concept?

3. Imagine that you are opening a small restaurant and need to hire several servers, cooks, and delivery people. The other restaurants in the neighborhood pay only a few dollars an hour (in most cases, minimum-wage laws don't apply to employees who receive tips) and you know that the staff of these restaurants struggle to make a living—most are living below the poverty line, and many work second jobs. You don't feel comfortable paying such low wages, but are also worried about being able to compete with the other restaurants in the area. What do you do?

Biographies and Background Information

The **Talmud** is the Jewish oral law. It consists of two parts: the Mishnah (codified by 200 CE), which consists primarily of concise legal statements; and the Gemara (codified around the sixth century CE), which expands upon and comments on the Mishnah. The Talmud is divided into tractates (Hebrew: *masekhtot*), each of which deals primarily with a certain set of topics.

Rabbi Moshe ben Nachman (a.k.a. Nachmanides/Ramban, Spain, 1194–1270) was one of the most influential biblical commentators, as well as a mystic and philosopher.

Rabbi Shlomo ben Aderet (a.k.a. Rashba, Spain, 1235–1310) wrote thousands of *teshuvot* (responses to legal questions), as well as a commentary on the Talmud and other legal works.

Jonah Gerondi (Catalonia, d. 1263) is best known for his moral and ethical writings, including *Sefer haYirah*.

Discussion Questions for Chapter 5— Servants to Servants or Servants to God: Workers, Employers, and Unions

1. What was the best workplace situation you have ever experienced? What was the worst? Did these experiences correspond to the descriptions of good and bad workplaces in the Jewish texts cited in this chapter? Why or why not?

2. As Rabbi Jacobs notes, Jewish tradition is ambivalent about whether work is inherently valuable or a necessary evil. What do you think? When have you experienced work as inherently valuable? When have you experienced it as a necessary evil?

3. Rabbi Jacobs suggests that Jewish texts do not leave wages to the fluctuations of the market, but recommend regulating the market in order to guarantee wages that will allow workers to support their families. Do you agree with this conclusion? Why or why not?

4. In your own work experiences, when have you seen employers and employees follow the standards laid out in this chapter? When have you seen these standards not followed? What has been the result for the employers and employees in each situation?

6

They Shall Tremble No More: Housing and Homelessness

Goal

- Participants will understand some Jewish approaches to what makes a house secure and appropriate for human habitation.

Trigger Exercise

1. Pass out two sheets of paper to each participant, as well as markers or crayons. Ask participants to draw, on one page, a home that would feel secure to them. This drawing can be based on a real place that they have lived, or can be an imagined place. On the other page, participants should draw a home that would not feel secure to them. Again, this drawing can be based on a real experience, or on an imagined home. Emphasize to participants that this is not an art class—they should not feel constrained by their drawing abilities.

2. Ask a few participants to share one or both of their drawings. (In a larger group, you can ask participants to share in small groups or in pairs.) Ask participants to describe the factors that contribute to each of these homes feeling either secure or not secure.

3. Ask participants to share, either in the large group, or in pairs or threes: When have you felt the most secure in your living situation? When have you felt the least secure? What factors contributed to these feelings of security/insecurity?

Text Study

1. Babylonian Talmud, *Sukkah* 28b

ת״ר כל שבעת הימים אדם עושה סוכתו קבע וביתו עראי כיצד היו לו כלים
נאים מעלן לסוכה מצעות נאות מעלן לסוכה אוכל ושותה ומטייל בסוכה.

All seven days of Sukkot, you should treat the *sukkah* [temporary dwelling place] as your permanent home and your house as your temporary home. How should you do this? If you have nice dishes and serving platters, bring them into the *sukkah*; eat, drink and sleep in the *sukkah*.

2. Babylonian Talmud, *Sukkah* 2a–b

משנה סוכה שהיא גבוהה למעלה מעשרים אמה פסולה ורבי יהודה מכשיר
ושאינה גבוהה עשרה טפחים ושאין לה (שלשה) +מסורת הש״ס [שלש]+
דפנות ושחמתה מרובה מצלתה פסולה.

גמרא   רבא אמר מהכא (ויקרא כג) בסכת תשבו שבעת ימים אמרה תורה כל
שבעת הימים צא מדירת קבע ושב בדירת עראי עד עשרים אמה אדם עושה
דירתו דירת עראי למעלה מעשרים אמה אין אדם עושה דירתו דירת עראי אלא
דירת קבע אמר ליה אביי אלא מעתה עשה מחיצות של ברזל וסיכך על גבן הכי
נמי דלא הוי סוכה אמר ליה הכי קאאמינא לך עד עשרים אמה דאדם עושה
דירתו דירת עראי כי עביד ליה דירת קבע נמי נפיק למעלה מעשרים אמה דאדם
עושה דירתו דירת קבע כי עביד ליה דירת עראי נמי לא נפיק.

Mishnah: A *sukkah* that is higher than twenty cubits (between 31 and 38 feet) is invalid. Rabbi Yehuda says that it is valid. A *sukkah* that is less than ten handbreadths (between 2½ and 3 feet) high or that does not have at least three walls and whose sun is greater than its shade is invalid....

Rava said, "[The reason for the prohibition against a *sukkah* that is higher than twenty cubits is] that the Torah instructs us to dwell in Sukkot for seven days. This means: for all seven days, leave your permanent home and live in a temporary home. A person would build a temporary home that is up to twenty cubits high, but would not build a temporary home higher than twenty cubits." Abaye said, "By that logic, if one made walls of iron and placed *schach* (natural materials used for the covering of a *sukkah*), this also would not be considered a valid *sukkah*." Rava replied, "I would say to you that as long as it is lower than twenty cubits, even a permanent structure is considered a valid *sukkah*; if it is over twenty cubits, even if it is temporary, it is not a valid *sukkah*.

3. Maimonides, *Mishneh Torah, Hilkhot Tefillin u'Mezuzah* 1:1

עשרה תנאין יש בבית ואחר כך יתחייב הדר בו לעשות לו מזוזה, ואם חסר תנאי
אחד מהן פטור מן המזוזה ואלו הן: שיהיה בן ארבע אמות על ארבע אמות או
יתר, ושתהיינה לו שתי מזוזות, ויהיה לו משקוף, ותהיה לו תקרה, ויהיו לו
דלתות, ויהיה השער גבוה עשרה טפחים או יותר, ויהיה הבית חול, ויהיה עשוי
לדירת אדם, ועשוי לדירת כבוד, ועשוי לדירת קבע.

There are ten conditions that a house must meet in order for the resident to be obligated to put up a *mezuzah* [scroll], and if it fails to meet any one of these conditions, [the resident] is not obligated to put up a *mezuzah*, and these are they: It must be at least four amot by four amot. It must have two doorposts. It must have a lintel. It must have a roof. It must have doors. The gate must be ten *tefachim* [about 32 inches] or higher. It must be for ordinary purposes. It must be made as a place for people to live. It must be made as an honorable place [as opposed to, say, a bathroom]. It must be made as a permanent place.

4. Deuteronomy 22:8

כי תבנה בית חדש ועשית מעקה לגגך ולא תשים דמים בביתך כי יפל הנפל
ממנו:

When you build a new house, make a guardrail for your roof, so that you will not bring any blood guilt upon your house if anyone falls from it (Deuteronomy 22:8).

Questions for Discussion

1. According to these texts, what makes a structure a permanent home? What makes a structure an impermanent place to live?
2. What elements are necessary to make a home appropriate for human life? How do these elements compare with your experiences of what makes a home feel secure or insecure?

Biographies and Background Information

A **sukkah** is a temporary dwelling place built for the holiday of Sukkot. The *sukkah* represents the temporary structures in which the Israelites are said to have lived during their journey from Egyptian slavery to freedom in the Promised Land. In addition, the *sukkah* reminds us of the huts in which farmers would live during the harvest season in order to be as close as possible to their crops. During Sukkot, it is traditional to eat and even sleep in the *sukkah*.

A **mezuzah** is a scroll containing some biblical verses that Jews traditionally place on the doors of their homes, in order to literally carry out the commandment to write the words of the Torah "on the doorposts of your home." A *mezuzah* is only placed on the door of a place where people live permanently.

The **Talmud** is the Jewish oral law. It consists of two parts: the Mishnah (codified by 200 CE), which consists primarily of concise legal statements; and the Gemara (codified around the sixth century CE), which expands upon and comments on the Mishnah. The Talmud is divided into tractates (Hebrew: *masekhtot*), each of which deals primarily with a certain set of topics.

Maimonides (a.k.a. Rambam, Cordoba/Egypt, 1135–1204) is one of the best-known figures in Jewish philosophy and law. His major works include the *Mishneh Torah*, a restatement of Talmudic law aimed at ordinary Jews, and *Moreh Nevuchim*, a philosophical work in which he grapples with the major philosophical questions of the scholarly Arabic world of his day through a Jewish lens.

Discussion Questions for Chapter 6— They Shall Tremble No More: Housing and Homelessness

1. Rabbi Jacobs suggests that a person's housing situation can have a major effect on their health, happiness, and sense of security. Have you experienced or observed this phenomenon in your own life? In what situations?
2. How would you define adequate housing? What are your own minimum housing needs? How do these correspond to the definition of adequate housing presented in this chapter?
3. Who do you think is responsible for providing affordable housing? Individuals? Organizations? Local governments? The federal government?

7

I Will Remove Illness from Within Your Midst: The Provision of Health Care

Goal

- Participants will understand some Jewish approaches to providing health care.

Trigger Exercise

1. Tell participants that you are going to role play a call between a health insurance client and a staff member at the insurance agency. Ask for a volunteer to suggest a situation—this may be a situation that s/he has personally experienced, or one that s/he has heard about from friends or relatives. Examples include: trying to get a procedure covered or learning that the cost of a drug has gone up exponentially.
2. Ask for two volunteers to role play this situation the way they imagine it would take place today. They should feel free to be as creative as they want.
3. Ask for two new volunteers to role play how this situation would play out in an ideal world.
4. Ask participants to reflect on the two role plays they saw. What would need to change in order to move from a world in which the first happens to a world in which the second happens?

Text Study

1. *Shulchan Arukh, Yoreh De'ah* 249:16

יש מי שאומר שמצות בית הכנסת עדיפא ממצות צדקה, ומצות צדקה לנערים
ללמוד תורה או לחולים עניים, עדיף ממצות בית הכנסת.

There are those who say that the *mitzvah* of constructing a synagogue is more important than that of *tzedakah* [in general], and the *mitzvah* of giving *tzedakah* to youths to study Torah or to the poor among the sick is more important than that of constructing a synagogue.

2. Rabbi Eliezer Waldenburg, *Tzitz Eliezer* 5:4

מתקון הצבור בכל מקום ומקום שישראל יושבים, ליחד קופה לביקור חולים,
והוא שהחולים העניים שאין ידם משגת להוצאות רפואתם, הקהל שולחים להם
רופא לבקרם והרפואות מכיס הקהל ונותנים להם מזון הראוי לחולים דבר יום
ביומו כפי ציווי הרופאים.

It has been enacted that in every place in which Jews live, the community sets aside a fund for care of the sick. When poor people are ill and cannot afford medical expenses, the community sends them a doctor to visit them, and the medicine is paid for by the communal fund. The community gives them food appropriate for the ill, day by day, according to the directions of the doctor.

3. Rabbi Nissim ben Reuven of Gerona (Ran), *She'elot uteshuvot 1, Dibbur hamatchil "V'haben hayoresh"*

ובני העיר וגם בני החבורה שמא אין רשות בידם לשנות מקופה של הקדש
חולים לקופה של הקדש ת״ת, ועוד שהקדש החבורות נעשה בפירוש גם לעניי
עולם כמו לעניי העיר, והוי דומיא דבית הכנסת של כרכים שאין להם לבני העיר
רשות למכרה.

If the residents of the city or of a collective want to reallocate the fund for the sick to the fund to support students, they are not allowed to do so. Furthermore, the fund for the sick is explicitly for the poor of the world, just as for the poor of that town. In this respect, it is like the synagogue of a city, which the residents of that city do not have permission to sell.

4. Chaim David HaLevy, *Aseh L'cha Rav* 7:70 (trans. Rabbi David Ellenson, *After Emancipation: Jewish Religious Responses to Modernity*, 423)

וכיום חובה זאת היא פשוטה בכל מדינה מתקדמת, וכל מחוסר עבודה זכאי לביטוח לאומי לקיום מינימלי.

Today, this obligation is widespread among every advanced nation, and each person who lacks work is deemed worthy of national insurance [that will ensure] a minimal standard necessary for subsistence.

Questions for Discussion

1. According to these texts, who is responsible for providing health care? How should a community go about ensuring health care for all of its members?
2. How do these texts suggest allocating communal funds in such a way as to guarantee health care? What other priorities may compete for funding with the health care system?
3. If you were to create a health care system based on the principles derived from these texts, what would this health care system look like?

Biographies and Background Information

The **Shulchan Arukh** was written by Rabbi Joseph Caro (Israel, 1488–1575). The *Shulchan Arukh* is probably the most authoritative code of Jewish law.

Rabbi Eliezer Waldenburg (Jerusalem, 1917–2006) was a leading figure in the Israeli rabbinate. He is best known for his writings on medical ethics, and for taking courageous and often progressive positions on issues such as transsexuality and economics.

Rabbi Nissim ben Reuven of Gerona (Barcelona, 1320–80) was a legal authority who wrote a commentary on the Talmud, as well as many *teshuvot* (legal rulings).

Rabbi Chaim David HaLevy (Palestine/Israel, 1924–98) was the Sephardic chief rabbi of Tel Aviv from 1973 until his death. He wrote a significant number of legal rulings on economic issues.

Discussion Questions for Chapter 7—I Will Remove
Illness from Within Your Midst: The Provision of Health Care

1. Have you ever experienced a disruption in your own health care, or had a conflict with your insurance company over the provision of care? What was the impact of this experience on you?

2. A number of the texts included in this chapter describe God as personally feeling human pain. What might it mean to believe that human death or sickness negatively affects the divine image? How might that belief affect our attitudes toward health care?

3. This chapter notes that a number of players—including the doctor, patient, insurance company, community, and government—all bear some responsibility for the provision of health care. How would you describe the relative responsibilities of each of these parties?

4. If you were to create the ideal health care system, what would it look like? In what ways would this system resemble or differ from the vision laid out in this chapter?

8

The City and the Garden: Environmental Sustainability for the Twenty-first Century

Goal

- Participants will understand some Jewish approaches to addressing environmental issues in a sustainable and just way.

Trigger Exercise

1. Present participants with the following scenario. Ask them to work in pairs or small groups to draft a response.

Springfield, USA, has recently closed its local landfill, which was full, and has struck a deal with a town thirty miles away to send solid waste there. In order to make this system work, Springfield will have to build a new waste transfer station. Right now, there is a plan to place this waste transfer station in a low-income neighborhood on the edge of the city. The residents of this neighborhood are extremely upset about this plan—there is already one waste transfer station in the neighborhood, as well as a bus depot. As a result, there is heavy truck and bus traffic through the area; this traffic has probably contributed to the high asthma rate among neighborhood children. The residents of this neighborhood have organized to stop the construction of this waste transfer station, and are suggesting that the station be placed instead in a wealthy neighborhood that also has water access. The city has countered that there are already plans to build a waterfront hotel in this wealthy neighborhood, and that this hotel will create six hundred jobs, many of which will go to the residents of the low-income neighborhood.

Some have suggested that if the city recycles a greater percentage of its solid waste, there will not be a need to build a waste transfer station at all. However, an expanded recycling program will require increased truck traffic through the city, and will also require a new tax on all residents.

2. Have participants read and discuss the following texts. Ask participants to respond to the situation outlined above through the eyes of these texts.

Text Study

1. Maimonides, *Mishneh Torah*, *Hilkhot Nizkei Mamon* 12:1

החופר בור ברשות הרבים, ונפל לתוכו שור או חמור ומת, ואפילו היה הבור
מלא גיזות של צמר וכיוצא בהן הרי בעל הבור חייב לשלם נזק שלם, שנאמר
"בעל הבור ישלם (שמות כא,לד) ואחד שור וחמור או שאר מיני בהמה וחיה
ועוף, לא נאמר שור או חמור (שמות כא,לג) אלא בהווה.

If one digs a pit in the public domain, and an ox or a donkey falls in it and dies, even if the pit was full of wool or some such thing, the one who dug the pit is responsible for paying damages.

2. Maimonides, *Mishneh Torah*, *Hilkhot Nizkei Mamon* 12:8–9

בור של שני שותפין, ועבר עליו הראשון ולא כיסהו, והשני ולא כיסהו הראשון
חייב, עד שימסור דולייו לשני; ומשמסר דולייו לשני לדלות ממנו נפטר
הראשון, ונתחייב השני לכסותו.כיסהו הראשון, ובא השני ומצאו מגולה, ולא
כיסהו—השני חייב. ועד אימתי יהיה השני לבדו חייב עד שיידע הראשון
שהבור מגולה, וכדי שישכור פועלים ,ויכרות ארזים ויכסנו. וכל שימות בו
בתוך זמן זה, השני לבדו חייב בו; וכל שימות בו אחר זמן זה שניהן חייבין
לשלם, שהרי שניהן פשעו בו.

If a pit belongs to two partners, and one passes by and does not cover it, then the second passes by and does not cover it, the first is liable until he hands the cover to the second. From the time that the first hands the cover to the second to cover it, the first becomes exempt from liability, and the second becomes liable. If the first covers it, and the second passes by and finds it uncovered and doesn't cover it, the second is liable. Until when does the second alone remain liable? Until the first learns that the pit is uncovered and has time to hire workers and to uproot trees and to cover it. And if anyone/anything dies in the pit in the meantime, the second alone is liable. If anyone/anything dies in the pit after this time, both are liable since both were negligent.

3. Mishnah, *Bava Batra* 2:9–10

מרחיקין את הנבלות ואת הקברות ואת הבורסקי מן העיר חמשים אמה אין
עושין בורסקי אלא למזרח העיר רבי עקיבא אומר לכל רוח הוא עושה חוץ
ממערבה ומרחיק חמשים אמה ומרחיקין את המשרה מן הירק ואת הכרישין מן
הבצלים ואת החרדל מן הדבורים ורבי יוסי מתיר בחרדל.

We distance carcasses, graveyards, and tanneries fifty amot from the city. We only place tanneries to the east of a city. Rabbi Akiva says: we may place them in any direction, except for the west, and distance them fifty amot. We distance a soaking pit from [a neighbor's] vegetables, leeks from onions, and mustard from bees.

4. Deuteronomy 23:13–15

יג וְיָד תִּהְיֶה לְךָ, מִחוּץ לַמַּחֲנֶה; וְיָצָאתָ שָׁמָּה, חוּץ. יד וְיָתֵד תִּהְיֶה לְךָ, עַל-אֲזֵנֶךָ;
וְהָיָה, בְּשִׁבְתְּךָ חוּץ, וְחָפַרְתָּה בָהּ, וְשַׁבְתָּ וְכִסִּיתָ אֶת-צֵאָתֶךָ. טו כִּי יְהוָה אֱלֹהֶיךָ
מִתְהַלֵּךְ בְּקֶרֶב מַחֲנֶךָ, לְהַצִּילְךָ וְלָתֵת אֹיְבֶיךָ לְפָנֶיךָ, וְהָיָה מַחֲנֶיךָ, קָדוֹשׁ: וְלֹא-
יִרְאֶה בְךָ עֶרְוַת דָּבָר, וְשָׁב מֵאַחֲרֶיךָ:

Further, there shall be an area for you outside the camp, where you may relieve yourself. With your gear you shall have a spike, and when you have squatted you shall dig a hole with it and cover up your excrement. Since Adonai your God moves about in your camp to protect you and to deliver your enemies to you, let your camp be holy; let God not find anything unseemly among you and turn away from you.

5. Maimonides, *Mishneh Torah, Hilkhot Melakhim* 6:14

ואסור להיפנות בתוך המחנה, או על פני השדה בכל מקום; אלא מצות עשה
לתקן דרך שם מיוחדת להיפנות בה.

It is forbidden to relieve oneself inside the camp, or in the field anywhere. Rather, there is a positive commandment to create a specific place where people may relieve themselves.

Questions for Discussion

1. How do these texts suggest addressing the disposal of waste and the placement of potentially toxic businesses? How does this compare to how we ordinarily address these issues in our own society?
2. What guidelines do these texts offer for distributing responsibility for the public space, as well as burdens that arise within public space? How might we apply these guidelines to environmental concerns in our own society?

Biographies and Background Information

The **Talmud** is the Jewish oral law. It consists of two parts: the Mishnah (codified by 200 CE), which consists primarily of concise legal statements; and the Gemara (codified around the sixth century CE), which expands upon and comments on the Mishnah. The Talmud is divided into tractates (Hebrew: *masekhtot*), each of which deals primarily with a certain set of topics.

Maimonides (a.k.a. Rambam, Cordoba/Egypt, 1135–1204) is one of the best-known figures in Jewish philosophy and law. His major works include the *Mishneh Torah*, a restatement of Talmudic law aimed at ordinary Jews, and *Moreh Nevuchim*, a philosophical work in which he grapples with the major philosophical questions of the scholarly Arabic world of his day through a Jewish lens.

Discussion Questions for Chapter 8—The City and the Garden: Environmental Sustainability for the Twenty-first Century

1. To what extent do you think about the environmental impact of your everyday activities? How has your consciousness about environmental impact changed at all in the recent past? How has your behavior changed?
2. Rabbi Jacobs comments, "Judaism makes clear that the health of humanity and of the natural world depend deeply on one another." In what ways have you experienced that interdependence succeed or fail?
3. Rabbi Jacobs argues that human beings have a responsibility to act as stewards of the world's resources in order to create a more sustainable society. How might the concept of stewardship help us think about the appropriate distribution of resources and responsibility?
4. Rabbi Jacobs asks whether Judaism favors urban life, rural life, or views the two as equally valid. How would you answer this question? Have you ever taken environmental concerns into account when deciding where to live? If so, what decision did you make as a result?

9

When Your Brother Is Flogged:
Crime, Punishment, and Rehabilitation

Goal

- Participants will understand some Jewish approaches to addressing the question of how and when to use prison as punishment.

Trigger Exercise

Ask participants to respond to one or more of the following questions, either in pairs or in the full group:

1. Have you ever had an experience with the criminal justice and/or prison system? What was this experience like? What did it teach you about criminal justice?

2. What associations do you have with the word "prison"? What feelings does this word evoke in you?

3. Imagine that you are serving on a jury in the case of a small-scale drug dealer. You believe that there is evidence to convict the defendant, but you know that, according to your state's mandatory sentencing laws, this will mean a minimum prison sentence of five years—being sentenced to treatment is not an option. You are concerned about this person being let back on the street, where he is likely to resume his drug trade, but also doubt that time in prison will result in his changing careers. What do you do?

Text Study

1. Numbers 15: 32–35

לב וַיִּהְיוּ בְנֵי-יִשְׂרָאֵל, בַּמִּדְבָּר; וַיִּמְצְאוּ, אִישׁ מְקֹשֵׁשׁ עֵצִים בְּיוֹם הַשַּׁבָּת. לג
וַיַּקְרִיבוּ אֹתוֹ, הַמֹּצְאִים אֹתוֹ מְקֹשֵׁשׁ עֵצִים—אֶל-מֹשֶׁה, וְאֶל-אַהֲרֹן, וְאֶל, כָּל-
הָעֵדָה. לד וַיַּנִּיחוּ אֹתוֹ, בַּמִּשְׁמָר: כִּי לֹא פֹרַשׁ, מַה-יֵּעָשֶׂה לוֹ. לה וַיֹּאמֶר יְהוָה
אֶל-מֹשֶׁה, מוֹת יוּמַת הָאִישׁ; רָגוֹם אֹתוֹ בָאֲבָנִים כָּל-הָעֵדָה, מִחוּץ לַמַּחֲנֶה.

Once, when the Israelites were in the wilderness, they came upon a man gathering wood on
the Sabbath day. Those who found him as he was gathering wood brought him before Moses,
Aaron, and the whole community. He was placed in custody (*mishmar*), for it had not been
specified what should be done to him. Then Adonai said to Moses, "The man shall be put to
death: the whole community shall pelt him with stones outside the camp." So the whole community took him outside the camp and stoned him to death—as Adonai had commanded
Moses.

2. Babylonian Talmud, *Brakhot* 54b

אמר רב יהודה אמר רב ארבעה צריכין להודות יורדי הים הולכי מדברות ומי
שהיה חולה ונתרפא ומי שהיה חבוש בבית האסורים ויצא ... מי שהיה חבוש
בבית האסורין מנלן דכתיב יושבי חשך וצלמות וגו' כי המרו אמרי אל וגו'
ואומר ויכנע בעמל לבם וגו' ואומר ויזעקו אל ה'.

Rabbi Yehuda said in the name of Rav: There are four types of people who need to give
thanks: Those who go down to the sea; those who cross over the desert; one who was sick
and was healed; and one who was imprisoned and was released ... how do we know that one
who was imprisoned should give thanks? It says, "Those who sit in darkness and shadow,
being bound in affliction and iron" (Psalms 107:10) and "For they have rebelled against the
words of God, etc." (ibid., verse 11) and it says, "Therefore, God humbled their heart with
travail, etc." (ibid. verse 12) and it says, "They cried out to God in their trouble, and God
saved them from distress" (ibid., verse 13).

3. *Tosefta, Sanhedrin* 12:7

מתרין בו ושותק מתרין בו והרכין בראשו מתרין בו פעם ראשונה ושניה
ובשלישית כונסין אותו לכיפה אבא שאול אומר אף בשלישית מתרין בו
וברביעית כונסין אותו לכיפה ונותנין לו לחם צר ומים לחץ כיוצא בו חייבי
מלקות שלקו ושנו מלקין אותן פעם ראשונה ושניה ובשלישית כונסין אותן
לכיפה אבא שאול אומר אף בשלישית מלקין אותן וברביעית כונסין אותן
לכיפה ומאכילין אותן שעורים עד שכריסן נבקעת.

He is warned once and is silent; he is warned again and indicates consent. If he is warned a first, then a second time, the third time, he is placed in the *kippah* [small cell]. Abba Shaul says, "Even the third time, we warn him, and the fourth time, he is placed in the *kippah*." And we feed him minimal bread and water.

This is the rule for those who are liable for lashes and who repeat the crime: We give them lashes a first, then a second time; the third time, they are placed in the *kippah*. Abba Shaul says, "Also the third time, we give them lashes, and the fourth time, they are placed in the *kippah*." And we feed him barley until his stomach bursts.

4. Maimonides, *Mishneh Torah, Hilkhot Rotzeach Ush'mirat Hanefesh* 2:5

הרי בית דין חייבין מכל מקום להכותם מכה רבה הקרובה למיתה, ולאסור אותן
במצור ובמצוק שנים רבות, ולצערן בכל מיני צער : כדי להפחיד ולאיים על
שאר הרשעים, שלא יהיה להם הדבר לפוקה ולמכשול לבב, ויאמר הריני מסבב
להרוג אויבי כדרך שעשה פלוני, ואיפטר.

The court is obligated, in any case, to punish them with a serious punishment, close to death, and to confine them in a small and narrow place for many years, and to afflict them with all sorts of afflictions in order to instill fear in other wicked people, so that the incident will not become an obstacle or a stumbling block, such that another person will say, "I will bring about the death of my enemy as so-and-so did, and I will go free."

5. Rabbi Ben-Zion Meir Chai Uziel, *Piskei Uziel b'She'elot Hazman, Siman* 30

כל זמן שהיושב בו נמצא בבית האסורין ושניהם בעל בית האסורים והאסיר
מצפים לשעה שיותר אסיר זה ממאסרו לפנות את החדר, הלכך חשוב כבית
שלא הוקבע לדירה דומיא דבתים שבספינה שאינם אלא לזמן הנסיעה.

The entire time that one dwells in the prison, both the prisoner and the administrator of the prison wait for the moment when the prisoner will be released and the cell will be vacated; therefore, it is thought of as a home that is not established as a permanent dwelling, similar to homes on ships.

6. Rabbi Meshulam Rath, *Kol Mevaser* 1:83

ובדרך כלל לבי מהסס נגד חוק בהסכמת הרבנים למאסר קצוב של חמש או שלש שנים בתור עונש על חטא שעבר שלא נמצא כזה בחוקי ההלכה שלנו, רק מאסר זמני בתור אמצעי של כפייה או שמירה . . . או כניסה לכיפה בהורג נפש שלא בהתראה וזו הלכה למשה מסיני היא.

In general, I am hesitant about the agreement of the Rabbis regarding imprisonment of five or three years as punishment for sin, for nothing like this is present in our *halakhah*—rather, we have only temporary imprisonment in order to force compliance, or to hold a person [until the trial is completed] … or placement in the *kippah* for a murderer who was not warned [ahead of time about the consequences of his/her act, as is a necessary condition for carrying out capital punishment]. And this is a law given to Moses at Sinai.

Questions for Discussion

1. How do these texts understand the function and purpose of imprisonment? How is this similar to or different from the way in which our society thinks about the purpose of prison?
2. When, according to these texts, is prison necessary? How does this correspond to our society's decisions about when to imprison someone?
3. If you were to design a prison system that reflects these texts, what would it look like? How would it be similar to or different from our current prison system?

Biographies and Background Information

The **Talmud** is the Jewish oral law. It consists of two parts: the Mishnah (codified by 200 CE), which consists primarily of concise legal statements; and the Gemara (codified around the sixth century CE), which expands upon and comments on the Mishnah. The Talmud is divided into tractates (Hebrew: *masekhtot*), each of which deals primarily with a certain set of topics.

The *Tosefta* is a compilation of rabbinic law codified around the late first or second century CE. It often parallels the Mishnah, and has some historical relationship to the Mishnah.

Maimonides (a.k.a. Rambam, Cordoba/Egypt, 1135–1204) is one of the best-known figures in Jewish philosophy and law. His major works include the *Mishneh Torah*, a restatement of Talmudic law aimed at ordinary Jews, and *Moreh Nevuchim*, a philosophical work in which he grapples with the major philosophical questions of the scholarly Arabic world of his day through a Jewish lens.

Rabbi Ben-Zion Meir Chai Uzziel (Israel, 1880–1953) served in a number of key positions in Palestine/Israel, including the Chacham Bashi (chief rabbi recognized by the Turkish government) from 1911 until WWI; chief rabbi of Tel Aviv (1923–1939); and Sephardic chief rabbi of Israel (1939 until his death).

Rabbi Meshulam Rath (Ukraine/Romania/Israel, 1875–1962) was a prominent *halakhic* authority whose most famous work was *Kol Mevaser*. He was deeply involved in the religious Zionist movement, and eventually made his home in Israel.

Discussion Questions for Chapter 9— When Your Brother Is Flogged: Crime, Punishment, and Rehabilitation

1. Have you had personal experience with the criminal justice system? If so, what was this experience like? How, if at all, did the experience change your views of the criminal justice system?
2. According to Rabbi Jacobs, Jewish law distinguishes between violent crimes and other types of misbehavior, such as property crimes. What value does this categorization suggest? Do you agree with this value? Why or why not?
3. Many of the texts included in this chapter indicate a simultaneous concern for the safety and welfare of the victim and for the humanity of the perpetrator. What relative weight would you give to each of these concerns? How might you suggest that contemporary criminal justice law take into account both of these concerns?
4. How would you describe the ideal criminal justice system? In what ways would this system correspond to or differ from the ideals outlined in this chapter?

CONCLUSION

Judaism in the Public Sphere

Goal

- Participants will articulate their own approach to bringing their Judaism into the public sphere.

Trigger Exercise

1. Ask participants what comes to mind when they hear the term "religion in the public square." Instruct them to write their associations on the board or on a flip chart.
2. Have participants look at this list. Ask them whether these associations evoke primarily positive or negative feelings for them.
3. Read the text below, or a longer excerpt from the Conclusion of *There Shall Be No Needy: Pursuing Social Justice through Jewish Law and Tradition*. Ask participants whether they agree or disagree with this vision of Judaism in the public square. Why?

Text Study

1. Jill Jacobs, *There Shall Be No Needy: Pursuing Social Justice through Jewish Law & Tradition*, pp. 219–221

Many individual Jews play prominent roles in public life, as community organizers, public policy experts, legislators, and government officials.... At the same time, many Jewish organizations are deeply engaged in policy debates at local, state, national, and international levels.

What is missing in much of this work is a real public discussion about how Jewish law and tradition might address contemporary policy questions. Those on either side of an issue often quote texts to support their points, but they do so in a way that does not invite debate or discussion. Instead, when Jews engage in the public discourse as Jews, we should bring Jewish law and principles into the conversation in such a way as to enrich, rather than shut down, the discourse.

If we succeed in facilitating this rich conversation, we will create a new kind of Jewish politics in America. Rather than trade sound bites, we will continue the Talmudic tradition of dialogue, in which various questioners and commentators engage in an often messy conversation that eventually leads to a fuller understanding of the situation at hand.... We will witness the emergence of a Judaism that views ritual observance, study, and engagement in the world as an integrated whole, rather than as separate and distinct practices. The Jewish community's deepened involvement in public life will change the face of religious politics in America, as other communities will recognize the Jewish community as an important and authentic religious voice in the public square of America.

Questions for Discussion

1. What role do you think religion should play in the public sphere? How could Jews bring Jewish law into public policy discussions?
2. What role do you think religious people should play in public life? Should they speak from their religious values? If so, how?
3. Rabbi Jacobs lays out three essential principles: the dignity of human life; an attempt to rectify major disparities in power; and the mutual responsibilities between the individual and the community. How might these three principles inform the discussion of other public policy issues?

BIBLIOGRAPHY

Ellenson, David. *After Emancipation: Jewish Religious Responses to Modernity*. New York: Hebrew Union College, 2004.

Fine, Lawrence. *Physician of the Soul, Healer of the Cosmos: Isaac Luria and His Kabbalistic Fellowship*. Palo Alto: Stanford University Press, 2003.

RABBI JILL JACOBS is rabbi-in-residence at Jewish Funds for Justice, a national public foundation dedicated to mobilizing the resources of American Jews to combat the root causes of domestic social and economic injustice. She was named to *Forward's* list of fifty influential Jews, *Jewish Week's* list of "thirty-six under thirty-six," and *Newsweek's* "Top Fifty Rabbis List." She received rabbinic ordination and an MA in Talmud and Rabbinics from The Jewish Theological Seminary, and holds an MS in Urban Affairs from Hunter College. She is the author of *There Shall Be No Needy: Pursuing Social Justice through Jewish Law & Tradition* (Jewish Lights).

Also Available

The Way Into *Tikkun Olam* (Repairing the World)
By Rabbi Elliot N. Dorff, PhD
An accessible introduction to the Jewish concept of the individual's responsibility to care for others and repair the world. A finalist for the National Jewish Book Award.
6 x 9, 304 pp, Quality PB, 978-1-58023-328-6; 6 x 9, 320 pp, Hardcover, 978-1-58023-269-2

The Wisdom of Judaism
An Introduction to the Values of the Talmud
By Rabbi Dov Peretz Elkins
Explores the essence of Judaism through reflections on the words of the rabbinic sages and offers advice for life's most intractable dilemmas.
6 x 9, 192 pp, Quality PB, 978-1-58023-327-9

Also Available
The Wisdom of Judaism Teacher's Guide
8½ x 11, 18 pp, PB, 978-1-58023-350-7

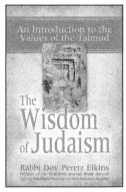

Praise for There Shall Be No Needy: Pursuing Social Justice through Jewish Law & Tradition

"A landmark work…. A model for how informed Jewish discourse on issues in the public square ought to take place. Required reading for all persons interested in what Judaism has to say on matters of social and public import. I cannot recommend it highly enough."
—**Rabbi David Ellenson**, president, Hebrew Union College–Jewish Institute of Religion

"A welcome new voice to the field of Jewish social justice. An important contribution to the debate on what Judaism has to say about the most important public issues of our day."
—**Rabbi Sidney Schwarz**, author, *Judaism and Justice: The Jewish Passion to Repair the World;* founder and president, PANIM: The Institute for Jewish Leadership and Values

"Groundbreaking and urgently needed…. A timely and profoundly insightful contribution to a growing literature on Jewish social justice."　　　　　—**Rabbi Sharon Brous**, IKAR

"[From] one of the most gifted Jewish thinkers and activists of our generation…. A must-read for all concerned with the future of Judaism and its role in the healing of the world."
—**Rabbi Or N. Rose**, director, Interfaith & Social Justice Initiatives, Hebrew College; coeditor, *Righteous Indignation: A Jewish Call for Justice*

JEWISH LIGHTS Publishing
www.jewishlights.com

Printed in the USA
CPSIA information can be obtained
at www.ICGtesting.com
JSHW060049150824
68134JS00031B/2683

9 781580 234290